New England Clam Chowder Recipes

A Savory Journey Through Classic and Creative Chowder Creations

While every precaution has been taken in the preparation of this book, the publisher assumes no responsibility for errors or omissions, or for damages resulting from the use of the information contained herein.

NEW ENGLAND CLAM CHOWDER RECIPES

First edition. February 8, 2024.

Copyright © 2024 Sammy Andrews.

ISBN: 979-8224834549

Written by Sammy Andrews.

Table of Contents

Sammy Andrews

Chapter 1: Introduction to Clam Chowder

Clam chowder, with its rich and creamy goodness, holds a special place in the hearts and palates of food lovers around the world. In this chapter, we embark on a culinary journey to discover the essence of clam chowder and its enduring appeal. From its humble beginnings to its status as a beloved comfort food, clam chowder has a story worth savoring.

The History and Origins of Clam Chowder

The roots of clam chowder can be traced back to the early days of American colonial history. The dish's exact origin remains a subject of debate, but it's clear that it emerged as a hearty and satisfying meal for New England settlers. These early chowders often featured simple ingredients like clams, salt pork, potatoes, and onions, all cooked together in a single pot.

As time passed, chowder recipes evolved to reflect the ingredients available in different regions of New England. In the coastal towns of Massachusetts, Rhode Island, and Maine, clams were abundant, leading to the creation of New England clam chowder. Rhode Island, in particular, favored a clear, broth-based chowder, while Massachusetts embraced the creamy, milk-based version that is now synonymous with New England clam chowder.

Regional Variations in Chowder

New England clam chowder is just one variation of this iconic dish. Throughout the United States, you'll find regional chowders that showcase local flavors and ingredients. For example:

Manhattan Clam Chowder: Known for its vibrant red color, Manhattan clam chowder swaps the creamy base for a tomato broth. It features a medley of vegetables like tomatoes, carrots, and celery, offering a brighter and slightly tangy flavor compared to its New England counterpart.

Rhode Island Clam Chowder: Rhode Island chowder, also known as "clear chowder," is light and brothy, highlighting the briny goodness of clams. It typically includes a combination of clams, potatoes, onions, and bacon for added flavor.

Minorcan Clam Chowder: Hailing from Florida's St. Augustine region, this spicy chowder incorporates datil peppers, a unique local ingredient. It's a testament to how diverse and inventive chowder recipes can be.

The Appeal of New England Clam Chowder

What makes New England clam chowder so irresistible? It's a combination of factors that come together in each velvety spoonful. Here's why so many people adore it:

Creamy Comfort: New England clam chowder offers a creamy, indulgent base that warms the soul on even the chilliest of days. The smooth texture is a comforting contrast to the tender clams and hearty potatoes.

Perfect Pairings: It's no secret that chowder and fresh-baked bread or oyster crackers are a match made in culinary heaven. The dunkability factor enhances the overall experience.

Adaptability: While the classic recipe remains a favorite, New England clam chowder is also a canvas for creativity. You can experiment with ingredients and flavors to suit your taste and dietary preferences.

Now that we've set the stage for our clam chowder journey, let's dive into the heart of this beloved dish by exploring its essential elements, starting with the star ingredient: clams. In Chapter 3, we'll delve into the world of clams, discussing the types used in chowder, how to source and handle them, and the art of shucking and preparing clams for your culinary creations.

Chapter 2: The Essence of New England Clam Chowder

In this chapter, we'll take a deep dive into the very heart and soul of New England clam chowder. What defines this classic dish, what sets it apart from other chowders, and the key flavor profiles and textures that make it so irresistible will be explored in detail.

Defining the Classic New England Chowder

New England clam chowder is an iconic American dish renowned for its simplicity and comforting flavors. At its core, it is characterized by several defining features:

Clams: The star of the show, clams, provide the rich, briny essence that infuses every bite of the chowder.

Creaminess: New England clam chowder is known for its creamy, milk-based broth. This luscious base serves as a backdrop to the tender clams, creating a velvety texture that coats the palate.

Potatoes: To add a hearty and satisfying element, New Englanders traditionally include diced potatoes in their chowder. These potatoes not only provide substance but also absorb the flavorful broth.

Onions: Sweet or mild onions are often used to add a subtle yet essential layer of flavor. They complement the clams and potatoes beautifully.

Bacon or Salt Pork: A touch of smoky, salty goodness from bacon or salt pork is a common addition, lending a savory depth to the chowder.

Seasonings: Common seasonings include black pepper, thyme, and bay leaves. These herbs and spices enhance the overall flavor profile without overpowering the clams.

What Sets New England Clam Chowder Apart

New England clam chowder stands out for several reasons, distinguishing it from other chowder variations:

Creaminess vs. Tomato-Based: While other chowders like Manhattan clam chowder opt for a tomato-based broth, New England clam chowder relies on a creamy base, creating a silky, soothing texture that's incredibly satisfying.

Mild and Savory: The creamy base, combined with the mild sweetness of onions and the brininess of clams, results in a well-balanced, savory dish that appeals to a wide range of tastes.

The Chowder's Aesthetic: With its pale, creamy hue punctuated by chunks of clams, potatoes, and bits of bacon, New England clam chowder has an inviting and rustic appearance.

Key Flavor Profiles and Textures

To truly appreciate New England clam chowder, it's essential to savor the key flavor profiles and textures that come together in each spoonful:

Brininess: The clams impart a delightful brininess that reflects the sea's essence. It's a reminder of the dish's coastal origins.

Creamy Smoothness: The creamy base envelops your taste buds, creating a luxurious mouthfeel that's both comforting and indulgent.

Hearty and Satisfying: Chunks of tender clams and soft potatoes add substance to the chowder, making it a filling and hearty meal.

Subtle Sweetness: The sweetness of onions, while not overpowering, adds depth and complexity to the overall flavor profile.

As we continue our exploration of New England clam chowder, we'll move on to Chapter 3, where we'll dive into the world of clams. We'll discuss the types of clams used in chowder, how to source and handle them, and the art of shucking and preparing clams to ensure that your chowder is nothing short of perfection.

Chapter 3: Clams: The Heart of the Chowder

In this chapter, we'll delve into the world of clams, the essential ingredient that gives New England clam chowder its distinct character. We'll explore the types of clams commonly used in chowder, how to source and handle them, and provide valuable tips for shucking and preparing clams to ensure your chowder is brimming with delicious, tender morsels.

Types of Clams Used in Chowder

The choice of clams is a crucial element in crafting the perfect clam chowder. Several types of clams are favored by chowder enthusiasts, each offering its unique flavor and texture:

Quahogs: These hard-shell clams come in various sizes, from littlenecks to cherrystones and chowder clams. Littlenecks are the smallest and most tender, while chowder clams are larger and ideal for heartier chowders.

Razor Clams: Long and slender, razor clams are known for their sweet, delicate flavor. They are less commonly used in chowder but can add a unique twist to your recipe.

Surf Clams: Often used in commercial clam chowder, surf clams are large and have a slightly chewy texture. They're perfect for those who enjoy substantial clam pieces in their chowder.

Steamers: Soft-shell clams, or steamers, are prized for their sweet and briny taste. They are typically used in chowders when you desire a particularly tender and succulent clam.

Sourcing and Handling Fresh Clams

To ensure the freshness and quality of your clams, consider the following tips when sourcing and handling them:

Choose Reputable Suppliers: Purchase clams from reputable seafood markets or suppliers known for their quality and freshness. Look for certifications and ask about the source of the clams.

Live Clams: When buying clams, they should be alive. Live clams will have tightly closed shells or may slightly open when tapped but should quickly close when touched. Avoid clams with open shells that don't close when tapped, as they may be dead and unsafe to eat.

Storage: Store live clams in the refrigerator in a breathable container, like a mesh bag or a bowl covered with a damp cloth. Keep them cold, but not submerged in water.

Rinse and Scrub: Before using clams, rinse them under cold running water to remove any sand or debris. Use a brush to scrub the shells gently. Discard any clams with damaged or cracked shells.

Tips for Shucking and Preparing Clams

Shucking clams can be a rewarding yet somewhat tricky task. Here are some tips to help you shuck and prepare clams with confidence:

Safety First: Use a sturdy, sharp knife and wear protective gloves to avoid accidental cuts. Place a folded kitchen towel on your work surface to stabilize the clam.

Opening the Clam: Insert the knife into the clam's hinge, where the two shell halves meet. Apply gentle pressure and wiggle the knife to pry the shells apart. Be patient and careful to avoid injuring yourself.

Separate and Clean: Once the clam is open, carefully separate the meat from the shell. Remove any residual sand or grit, and trim away any tough or dark parts. Cut the clam meat into bite-sized pieces for your chowder.

By mastering the art of selecting, handling, and preparing clams, you'll be well on your way to creating a clam chowder that highlights the natural flavors and textures of these ocean gems.

Chapter 4: Essential Ingredients and Equipment

In this chapter, we'll explore the foundational elements of crafting New England clam chowder—essential ingredients and the kitchen tools and equipment you'll need to achieve chowder perfection. We'll also discuss how to stock your chowder pantry to ensure you're always ready to whip up a satisfying bowl of chowder.

Common Chowder Ingredients

Before you embark on your clam chowder adventure, it's crucial to familiarize yourself with the common ingredients that will go into your delicious creation:

1. Clams: As we discussed in Chapter 3, the heart of clam chowder is, of course, the clams. Select the type that suits your taste and availability.

2. Potatoes: Potatoes add substance and a comforting starchiness to the chowder. Yukon Gold or Russet potatoes are excellent choices for their creamy texture.

3. Onions: Sweet or mild onions, such as Vidalia or yellow onions, provide a delicate sweetness and aromatic base for your chowder.

4. Bacon or Salt Pork: For a savory depth of flavor, many chowder recipes call for bacon or salt pork. These ingredients infuse a smoky, salty essence into the broth.

5. Dairy: Dairy is essential for achieving that creamy chowder texture. You'll need milk or half-and-half, and in some recipes, heavy cream.

6. Broth: While the clams themselves provide a significant amount of liquid, additional clam juice or seafood stock can be used to enhance the chowder's flavor.

7. Seasonings: Black pepper, thyme, and bay leaves are common seasonings to impart a subtle herbal complexity.

8. Butter: Some recipes incorporate butter to sauté onions and add richness to the chowder.

Kitchen Tools and Equipment You'll Need

To prepare a delightful bowl of clam chowder, you'll require the right kitchen tools and equipment. Here's what you'll need:

1. Chef's Knife and Cutting Board: A sharp chef's knife and a sturdy cutting board are essential for chopping vegetables, clams, and other ingredients.

2. Soup Pot or Dutch Oven: A large, heavy-bottomed pot is ideal for cooking your chowder. A Dutch oven is a popular choice due to its heat distribution.

3. Wooden Spoon or Whisk: These utensils are handy for stirring and combining ingredients without damaging the pot's surface.

4. Measuring Cups and Spoons: Accurate measurements are crucial for achieving consistent results.

5. Ladle: A ladle makes it easy to serve your chowder without spills.

6. Strainer or Colander: Useful for draining clams and any other ingredients that require it.

Stocking Your Chowder Pantry

To be ready to whip up clam chowder whenever the craving strikes, consider stocking your pantry with these essential items:

1. Canned Clams: Keep a supply of canned or jarred clams on hand for convenience, especially when fresh clams aren't readily available.

2. Clam Juice or Seafood Stock: These are great for boosting the clam flavor in your chowder.

3. Potatoes: Store potatoes in a cool, dark place, and they'll be ready when you are.

4. Onions: Onions have a long shelf life, making them a pantry staple.

5. Canned Bacon or Salt Pork: Having these on hand means you're always prepared to add that savory touch.

6. Long-Lasting Dairy: Consider powdered milk or canned evaporated milk for extended shelf life.

7. Seasonings and Herbs: Stock up on dried black pepper, thyme, and bay leaves, as well as any other favorite seasonings.

With these common ingredients and essential kitchen tools at your disposal, you'll be well-equipped to embark on your clam chowder cooking journey. In Chapter 5, we'll dive into the heart of chowder-making with a step-by-step guide to creating the classic New England clam chowder.

Chapter 5: Classic New England Clam Chowder

In this chapter, we'll explore the quintessential New England clam chowder—rich, creamy, and brimming with tender clams and potatoes. You'll find the traditional recipe with step-by-step instructions, valuable tips for achieving creamy perfection, and creative garnishing and serving suggestions to elevate your chowder experience.

Traditional Recipe and Step-by-Step Instructions

Ingredients:

- 2 dozen fresh littleneck or chowder clams (or equivalent canned clams)
- 4 slices of bacon, diced
- 1 large onion, finely chopped
- 3 cups peeled and diced Yukon Gold or Russet potatoes
- 2 cups clam juice or seafood stock
- 1 cup water
- 2 cups whole milk
- 1 bay leaf
- 1/2 teaspoon dried thyme
- Salt and black pepper to taste
- 2 tablespoons butter
- Chopped fresh parsley for garnish
- Oyster crackers or fresh-baked bread for serving

Instructions:

Prepare the Clams:

1. If using fresh clams, scrub them thoroughly to remove any sand or debris. Discard any clams with cracked or open shells that don't close when tapped.
2. Steam the fresh clams with water in a large covered pot until they open, about 5-7 minutes. Discard any clams that remain closed.

Shuck the Clams:

Once the clams are cool enough to handle, shuck them and coarsely chop the clam meat. Set aside.

Cook the Bacon:

In a large soup pot or Dutch oven, cook the diced bacon over medium heat until crispy. Remove the bacon with a slotted spoon and set it aside on a paper towel-lined plate.

Sauté the Onions:

In the same pot with the bacon fat, add the chopped onions and sauté until they become translucent and fragrant, about 5 minutes.

Add Potatoes and Liquid:

Add the diced potatoes, clam juice or seafood stock, and water to the pot. Bring to a simmer and cook until the potatoes are tender, about 10-15 minutes.

Create the Chowder Base:

Stir in the whole milk, bay leaf, and dried thyme. Simmer gently for another 10 minutes, being careful not to boil the mixture.

Blend in the Clams:

Add the chopped clams and simmer for an additional 5 minutes, or until the clams are heated through.

Season and Finish:

1. Remove the bay leaf and discard it.
2. Season the chowder with salt and black pepper to taste.
3. Stir in the butter to add richness and flavor.

Serve and Garnish:

1. Ladle the hot chowder into bowls.
2. Garnish each bowl with a sprinkle of crispy bacon and chopped fresh parsley.
3. Serve with oyster crackers or slices of fresh-baked bread.

Tips for Achieving Creamy Perfection

Achieving the perfect creamy texture for your New England clam chowder requires attention to detail. Here are some tips to help you reach that goal:

Avoid Boiling: Be cautious not to boil the chowder once the dairy has been added, as it can cause curdling. Keep the heat at a gentle simmer.

Thickening Agents: If you prefer a thicker chowder, you can create a roux (a mixture of butter and flour) separately and gradually whisk it into the chowder to thicken the broth.

Consistency Control: Adjust the chowder's thickness by adding more clam juice, stock, or milk to achieve your desired consistency.

Garnishing and Serving Suggestions

To enhance the visual appeal and flavor of your classic clam chowder, consider these creative garnishing and serving ideas:

Fresh Herbs: Besides parsley, you can garnish with fresh chives, dill, or tarragon for added freshness and color.

Grated Cheese: A sprinkle of grated Parmesan or cheddar cheese can provide a delightful contrast to the creamy chowder.

Hot Sauce or Paprika: For a touch of heat and color, offer hot sauce or a pinch of smoked paprika at the table.

Crusty Bread Bowls: Serve the chowder in hollowed-out bread bowls for a rustic and charming presentation.

With this classic New England clam chowder recipe and the accompanying tips, you're ready to embark on a culinary journey that will delight your taste buds and warm your heart.

Chapter 6: Creamy vs. Tomato-Based Chowders

In this chapter, we'll dive into the delicious world of creamy and tomato-based chowders, exploring the unique characteristics of each variation. We'll help you choose the right base for your chowder and provide insight into the distinct flavor profiles and pairings associated with these delightful creations.

Exploring Cream-Based and Tomato-Based Variations

Cream-Based Chowders:

Creamy chowders, like the classic New England clam chowder, feature a rich and velvety base that's created with dairy products such as milk, half-and-half, or heavy cream. These chowders are known for their comforting, smooth texture and mild, savory flavors. The creamy base complements the sweetness of clams and the heartiness of ingredients like potatoes and bacon.

Tomato-Based Chowders:

Tomato-based chowders, typified by Manhattan clam chowder, depart from the creaminess of their counterparts. They boast a vibrant red hue and a tangy, tomato-infused broth. Tomatoes, often combined with vegetables like celery, carrots, and bell peppers, provide a zesty contrast to the brininess of clams. These chowders tend to be lighter and have a more pronounced acidic note.

Choosing the Right Base for Your Chowder

The choice between creamy and tomato-based chowders depends on your personal preferences and the flavors you crave. Here are some factors to consider when making your decision:

Creamy Chowders: opt for creamy chowders if you enjoy a rich, indulgent, and comforting bowl of soup. They are perfect for those who prefer a milder, more balanced flavor profile with a smooth and velvety texture.

Tomato-Based Chowders: Choose tomato-based chowders if you crave a tangy, slightly spicy, and vibrant soup. These chowders are lighter on the palate and can be a refreshing alternative, especially in warmer weather.

Variety: Don't limit yourself to just one type. Experiment with both creamy and tomato-based chowders to discover which one suits your mood and the occasion best.

Flavor Profiles and Pairings

Creamy Chowders:

Flavor Profile: Creamy chowders offer a harmonious blend of brininess from clams, the mild sweetness of onions, and the smoky, salty notes from bacon. The creamy base adds luxurious texture and a hint of buttery richness.

Pairings: Creamy chowders pair wonderfully with crusty bread, oyster crackers, or even a simple side salad. The creamy base complements the textures of freshly baked bread, making it an ideal dunking companion.

Tomato-Based Chowders:

Flavor Profile: Tomato-based chowders have a lively and tangy flavor profile with the natural sweetness of tomatoes. They often feature a medley of vegetables, contributing to a more complex and layered taste.

Pairings: Tomato-based chowders go well with a crusty baguette or a side of garlic bread. Their zesty and acidic notes benefit from the contrast of crunchy, toasted bread.

Chapter 7: Chowder from Scratch: Homemade Broth

In this chapter, we'll delve into the art of crafting chowder from scratch, starting with the foundation of a homemade broth. You'll learn how to create flavorful clam broth and use it to build a delicious chowder base. We'll also explore the advantages of homemade broth over store-bought options.

Crafting Flavorful Clam Broth

Homemade clam broth is the secret ingredient that elevates your chowder to new heights. It infuses your soup with a depth of flavor that's unparalleled. Here's how to craft a flavorful clam broth:

Ingredients for Clam Broth:

- 2 dozen fresh littleneck or chowder clams (or equivalent canned clams)
- 4 cups of water
- 1 bay leaf
- A few black peppercorns
- 1 onion, roughly chopped
- 2 cloves of garlic, smashed
- Optional: A stalk of celery, a carrot, and a sprig of fresh thyme for added flavor

Instructions:

Preparing the Clams:

If using fresh clams, scrub them thoroughly to remove sand or debris. Discard any clams with cracked or open shells that don't close when tapped.

Cooking the Clams:

1. In a large pot, add the water, bay leaf, peppercorns, chopped onion, garlic, and any optional vegetables or herbs.
2. Bring the water to a boil, then reduce the heat to a gentle simmer.
3. Add the clams to the pot, cover, and simmer for about 10-15 minutes, or until the clams open.
4. Remove the open clams with a slotted spoon and set them aside. Discard any unopened clams.

Straining and Storing the Broth:

1. Strain the broth through a fine-mesh sieve or cheesecloth into a clean container.
2. Allow the broth to cool to room temperature before refrigerating it. Homemade clam broth can be stored in the refrigerator for up to three days or frozen for longer-term use.

Creating a Flavorful Chowder Base

With your homemade clam broth in hand, you're well on your way to creating a flavorful chowder base. Here's how to do it:

Ingredients for Chowder Base:

- 4 cups of homemade clam broth
- 2 cups of whole milk or half-and-half
- 2 tablespoons of butter
- 2 tablespoons of all-purpose flour (optional for thickening)
- Salt and black pepper to taste

Instructions:
Start with a Roux (Optional):

1. In a separate saucepan, melt the butter over medium heat.
2. Add the flour and whisk continuously to create a roux. Cook the roux for a few minutes until it turns a light golden color.

Combine Broth and Roux (Optional):

Gradually whisk the homemade clam broth into the roux, ensuring there are no lumps. Continue to whisk until the mixture thickens slightly.

Add Dairy and Seasonings:

1. Stir in the whole milk or half-and-half and heat the

mixture over low heat. Be careful not to bring it to a boil to prevent curdling.

2. Season the chowder base with salt and black pepper to taste. The clam broth will already have a natural saltiness, so adjust accordingly.

Homemade Broth vs. Store-Bought

While store-bought clam juice or seafood stock is a convenient option, crafting your own homemade broth has distinct advantages:

Flavor Control: Homemade broth allows you to control the flavor and quality of your chowder. You can adjust the seasoning and taste as you go, ensuring a rich and satisfying broth.

Freshness: Homemade broth is made from fresh clams and aromatics, delivering a fresher and more authentic taste than store-bought alternatives.

Cost-Effective: Making your own broth can be cost-effective, especially if you have access to fresh clams.

By crafting a flavorful clam broth and using it to create a chowder base, you're well on your way to chowder perfection.

Chapter 8: Chowder Base: Roux or Cream?

In this chapter, we'll explore the pivotal decision of whether to use roux or cream to create the chowder base. We'll delve into the roles each plays in chowder-making and provide insights into how to customize the thickness of your chowder to suit your preferences.

The Role of Roux in Chowder

Roux is a mixture of fat and flour used as a thickening agent in many culinary applications, including chowder. Here's how roux plays a role in your chowder base:

Thickening Power: Roux is excellent for thickening chowder. By whisking together melted butter and flour and gradually incorporating liquid (in this case, clam broth), you create a smooth, lump-free base with a consistent thickness.

Stability: Roux helps stabilize the chowder, preventing the separation of liquid and solids. It ensures a consistent, creamy texture throughout.

Flavor Enhancement: Depending on how long you cook the roux, it can develop a nutty aroma and add a subtle depth of flavor to your chowder.

To incorporate roux into your chowder base, follow these steps:

1. In a separate saucepan, melt butter over medium heat.
2. Add an equal amount of all-purpose flour to the melted butter.
3. Whisk continuously to create a smooth roux. Cook

until it reaches your desired level of color (from pale to golden brown).

4. Gradually whisk in your clam broth, creating a thickened base.
5. Combine the roux base with the other chowder ingredients and continue cooking as usual.

Using Cream to Thicken Your Chowder

Using cream as a thickening agent in chowder creates a luxurious and velvety texture. Here's how cream contributes to your chowder base:

Richness and Creaminess: Cream adds a luscious creaminess to the chowder without the need for roux. This is the hallmark of New England clam chowder and similar creamy chowders.

Flavor Enhancement: Cream enhances the overall richness and flavor of the chowder, complementing the sweetness of clams and other ingredients.

To use cream to thicken your chowder:

1. Combine your clam broth and other chowder ingredients (clams, potatoes, onions, etc.) in a pot.
2. Gradually pour in the cream and stir to combine.
3. Heat the mixture over low to medium heat, being careful not to bring it to a boil to prevent curdling.
4. Adjust the thickness by adding more cream or clam broth as needed.

Customizing Thickness to Your Preference

The choice between roux and cream is not a rigid one, and you can customize the thickness of your chowder according to your preferences:

For a Thicker Chowder: If you prefer a heartier and thicker chowder, use both roux and cream. Start by making a roux, then add cream to achieve your desired consistency. This method provides the best of both worlds: the stabilizing power of roux and the creamy richness of cream.

For a Lighter Chowder: To create a lighter chowder, rely solely on cream and skip the roux. Add cream gradually until you reach your desired thickness.

Balancing Act: Achieving the perfect thickness is a matter of balance. You can always adjust the consistency by adding more liquid (clam broth or cream) as you cook.

Ultimately, whether you choose roux or cream—or a combination of both—depends on your taste and the type of chowder you desire. The beauty of chowder-making lies in its flexibility, allowing you to customize every element to create a bowl that suits your palate perfectly.

Chapter 9: Chowder Variations from Coastal Towns

In this chapter, we'll embark on a flavorful journey to explore the diverse chowder specialties from iconic coastal destinations. We'll uncover unique ingredients and techniques that make each chowder distinct and provide insights on how to capture the essence of coastal flavors in your own kitchen.

Chowder Specialties from Iconic Coastal Destinations

Coastal towns and regions around the world have put their unique stamp on chowder, creating regional specialties that reflect local flavors and traditions. Here are some renowned chowder variations:

Rhode Island Clam Chowder: A clear broth clam chowder that lets the sweet and briny flavor of quahog clams shine. It often includes bacon, potatoes, and seasonings.

Minorcan Clam Chowder (Florida): Known for its spicy kick, this chowder incorporates datil peppers, which are native to the region. It's a tomato-based chowder with a hearty dose of heat.

Manhattan Clam Chowder: A vibrant, tomato-based chowder that features the bold flavors of New York. It includes clams, tomatoes, celery, carrots, and often a hint of spicy heat from red pepper flakes.

Hatteras Clam Chowder (North Carolina): This chowder uses a variety of seafood, including clams, shrimp, and fish. It's a tomato-based chowder with a coastal twist.

Pacific Northwest Clam Chowder (Washington and Oregon): Renowned for its use of local ingredients like Pacific razor clams, this creamy chowder incorporates potatoes and often includes smoky bacon.

Unique Ingredients and Techniques

Each coastal chowder variation is defined by its use of unique ingredients and techniques that capture the essence of the region. Here are some noteworthy elements to consider:

Local Seafood: Coastal chowders often feature seafood that's abundant in the region. From Pacific razor clams in the Pacific Northwest to quahogs in Rhode Island, the choice of clam or seafood can significantly impact the chowder's flavor.

Regional Produce: Incorporating locally sourced vegetables and herbs can elevate the chowder's flavor. For example, Minorcan Clam Chowder benefits from the use of datil peppers, while Pacific Northwest chowder may include local mushrooms.

Spices and Seasonings: Coastal chowders can vary in spiciness and flavor profile based on the regional spices and seasonings used. It's essential to understand the balance of spices for each variation.

Capturing Coastal Flavors at Home

To recreate the flavors of coastal chowders at home, follow these tips:

Research and Experiment: Study the chowder variations from your desired coastal destination. Look for authentic recipes and regional ingredients to use in your chowder.

Source Local Ingredients: Whenever possible, use locally sourced ingredients to capture the unique flavors of the region.

Balance Flavors: Pay attention to the balance of flavors, including the level of spiciness, acidity, and the interplay of ingredients. Adjust seasonings to match your taste preferences.

Embrace Creativity: Don't be afraid to put your spin on coastal chowder recipes. While tradition is important, adding a personal touch can make the chowder truly yours.

By exploring chowder specialties from iconic coastal destinations and incorporating regional ingredients and techniques, you can embark on a culinary adventure that brings the flavors of the coast to your own kitchen.

Chapter 10: Creative Twists: Seafood Medley Chowder

In this chapter, we'll venture into the world of creative chowder-making by exploring the delightful Seafood Medley Chowder. We'll learn how to incorporate a variety of seafood into your chowder, provide recipes for Seafood Medley Chowders, and delve into the art of balancing flavors and textures to create a harmonious seafood experience.

Incorporating a Variety of Seafood

A Seafood Medley Chowder is a celebration of the ocean's bounty, offering a diverse array of seafood flavors and textures. To craft a delicious Seafood Medley Chowder, consider using a combination of the following seafood options:

Clams: The star ingredient, clams bring a sweet and briny essence to the chowder.

Shrimp: Shrimp add a succulent, slightly sweet flavor and a tender bite.

Fish: Flaky white fish like cod or haddock can contribute a mild, delicate taste to the chowder.

Scallops: Scallops provide a buttery texture and a subtly sweet flavor.

Mussels: Mussels add a robust brininess to the chowder and absorb the flavors of the broth.

Lobster: Lobster meat, with its rich and slightly sweet taste, can be a luxurious addition.

Recipes for Seafood Medley Chowders

Here are two recipes for Seafood Medley Chowders to inspire your culinary creativity:

Recipe 1: Classic Seafood Medley Chowder
Ingredients:

- 1 pound of mixed seafood (clams, shrimp, fish, scallops, mussels, or lobster)
- 4 cups of clam broth
- 2 cups of whole milk or half-and-half
- 2 tablespoons of butter
- 1 onion, finely chopped
- 2 cloves of garlic, minced
- 2 cups of diced potatoes
- 1 bay leaf
- Salt and black pepper to taste
- Chopped fresh parsley for garnish

Instructions:

1. In a large pot, melt the butter over medium heat. Add the chopped onion and minced garlic. Sauté until they become fragrant and translucent.
2. Add the diced potatoes, clam broth, and bay leaf. Simmer until the potatoes are tender.
3. Stir in the whole milk or half-and-half.
4. Add the mixed seafood and simmer until they are cooked through, ensuring not to overcook.
5. Remove the bay leaf and discard it. Season the chowder with salt and black pepper to taste.
6. Garnish with chopped fresh parsley before serving.

Recipe 2: Mediterranean Seafood Medley Chowder
Ingredients:

- 1 pound of mixed seafood (clams, shrimp, fish, scallops, or mussels)
- 4 cups of seafood or vegetable broth
- 1 cup of white wine
- 1 onion, finely chopped
- 3 cloves of garlic, minced
- 1 red bell pepper, diced
- 1 zucchini, diced
- 1 cup of cherry tomatoes, halved
- 1 teaspoon of dried oregano
- 1/2 teaspoon of red pepper flakes (adjust to taste)
- Juice of 1 lemon
- Salt and black pepper to taste
- Chopped fresh basil for garnish

Instructions:

1. In a large pot, sauté the chopped onion and minced garlic in olive oil over medium heat until translucent.
2. Add the diced red bell pepper, zucchini, and cherry tomatoes. Sauté for a few minutes until the vegetables soften.
3. Pour in the white wine and allow it to simmer for a couple of minutes.
4. Add the seafood and dried oregano. Pour in the seafood or vegetable broth.
5. Simmer until the seafood is cooked through and the flavors meld together.

6. Season the chowder with red pepper flakes, lemon juice, salt, and black pepper.
7. Garnish with chopped fresh basil before serving.

Balancing Flavors and Textures

Creating a Seafood Medley Chowder that shines requires careful balancing of flavors and textures. Here are some tips:

Timing: Be mindful of cooking times for different seafood to prevent overcooking. Start with the seafood that takes the longest to cook and add the quicker-cooking varieties later.

Seasoning: Season the chowder judiciously to enhance the natural flavors of the seafood. Taste and adjust as needed.

Textures: Achieve a harmonious texture by balancing the tenderness of seafood with the creaminess of the broth and the bite of any added vegetables or potatoes.

Seafood Medley Chowders offer endless possibilities for culinary creativity. By exploring different combinations of seafood and flavor profiles, you can create chowders that cater to your unique tastes and capture the essence of the ocean in every spoonful.

Chapter 11: Vegetarian and Vegan Clam Chowder

In this chapter, we'll explore the world of vegetarian and vegan clam chowders, offering plant-based alternatives to the traditional seafood-based versions. You'll learn how to create rich, vegan cream bases and discover vegetarian protein substitutes that can replicate the flavors and textures of clams.

Plant-Based Clam Chowder Alternatives

Creating a vegetarian or vegan clam chowder involves replacing the traditional clams and clam broth with plant-based ingredients. Here are some alternatives:

Mushrooms: Mushrooms, especially oyster or shiitake varieties, can provide a similar umami-rich flavor and a meaty texture akin to clams.

Hearts of Palm: Hearts of palm, when thinly sliced or shredded, can mimic the texture of clam strips in chowder.

Seaweed or Kelp: Seaweed or kelp can impart a hint of oceanic flavor, reminiscent of the sea. Dulse, nori, or kombu are popular choices.

Vegetable Broth: Swap clam broth for vegetable broth to create a savory base for your chowder.

Creating Rich, Vegan Cream Bases

One of the signature elements of clam chowder is its creamy consistency. You can achieve a rich, vegan cream base using the following plant-based ingredients:

Coconut Milk: Full-fat coconut milk is a popular choice for creating a creamy and luscious base.

Cashews: Soaked and blended cashews can provide a velvety texture and a subtle nutty flavor.

Potatoes and Plant-Based Milk: Puree cooked potatoes with plant-based milk (such as almond or soy milk) to create a creamy, dairy-free base.

Silken Tofu: Silken tofu, when blended, can create a smooth and creamy texture suitable for chowder.

Vegetarian Protein Substitutes

To add protein to your vegetarian or vegan chowder, consider these options:

Plant-Based Proteins: Use plant-based proteins like tempeh, tofu, or seitan to replicate the protein content found in clams.

Legumes: Incorporate legumes such as white beans or chickpeas for added protein and a hearty texture.

Textured Vegetable Protein (TVP): TVP is a soy-based product that can mimic the texture of minced clams when rehydrated.

Recipe: Vegan Mushroom Clam Chowder
Ingredients:

- 8 oz of mushrooms (oyster or shiitake), finely chopped
- 1 onion, finely chopped
- 2 cloves of garlic, minced
- 2 cups of vegetable broth
- 1 cup of full-fat coconut milk
- 2 cups of diced potatoes
- 1 bay leaf
- 1/2 teaspoon of dried thyme

- Salt and black pepper to taste
- Chopped fresh parsley for garnish

Instructions:

1. In a large pot, sauté the chopped onion and minced garlic in olive oil over medium heat until translucent.
2. Add the diced potatoes, mushrooms, vegetable broth, bay leaf, and dried thyme. Simmer until the potatoes are tender.
3. Pour in the full-fat coconut milk and continue to simmer gently.
4. Season the chowder with salt and black pepper to taste.
5. Garnish with chopped fresh parsley before serving.

Creating vegetarian and vegan clam chowders allows you to enjoy the comforting flavors and textures of traditional chowder while aligning with dietary preferences or restrictions. By exploring plant-based alternatives and embracing creative ingredients, you can craft delicious chowders that cater to a variety of tastes and preferences.

Chapter 12: Healthy and Light Chowder Options

In this chapter, we'll explore ways to create healthy and light chowder options without compromising on flavor. You'll discover techniques for reducing calories and fat content, incorporating fresh vegetables, and find recipes for lighter broth-based chowders.

Reducing Calories and Fat Content

Enjoying a lighter chowder doesn't mean sacrificing flavor. Here are some strategies to reduce calories and fat content:

Use Low-Fat Dairy: Opt for low-fat or fat-free dairy options like skim milk or low-fat yogurt instead of full-fat alternatives. These can help reduce the overall fat content of your chowder.

Skip the Roux: Omitting the roux (butter and flour mixture) can significantly reduce the fat content in your chowder. Instead, rely on other thickening agents like pureed vegetables or reduced-fat dairy.

Lean Proteins: Choose lean proteins like skinless chicken, turkey, or lean cuts of pork instead of fatty meats like bacon or sausage.

Less Butter: Use less butter or a heart-healthy alternative like olive oil for sautéing vegetables.

Incorporating Fresh Vegetables

Including an abundance of fresh vegetables in your chowder not only boosts its nutritional value but also adds natural flavors and textures. Consider these vegetables for a healthier twist:

Celery: Celery adds a delightful crunch and a hint of freshness to your chowder.

Carrots: Carrots contribute natural sweetness and vibrant color to the dish.

Bell Peppers: Bell peppers offer a pop of color and a slightly sweet flavor.

Spinach or Kale: Leafy greens like spinach or kale provide a dose of nutrients and a pleasant earthy flavor.

Zucchini: Zucchini can add a light, summery touch to your chowder.

Lighter Broth-Based Chowder Recipes
Here are two recipes for lighter, broth-based chowders:
Recipe 1: Chicken and Vegetable Chowder
Ingredients:

- 1 lb of boneless, skinless chicken breast, diced
- 1 onion, finely chopped
- 2 cloves of garlic, minced
- 2 carrots, diced
- 2 celery stalks, diced
- 2 cups of diced potatoes
- 4 cups of chicken or vegetable broth (low-sodium)
- 2 cups of skim milk
- 1 bay leaf
- 1/2 teaspoon of dried thyme
- Salt and black pepper to taste
- Chopped fresh parsley for garnish

Instructions:

1. In a large pot, sauté the diced chicken until cooked through. Remove the chicken from the pot and set it aside.
2. In the same pot, sauté the chopped onion and minced garlic until translucent.
3. Add the diced carrots, celery, and potatoes. Sauté for a few minutes.
4. Pour in the chicken or vegetable broth, skim milk, bay leaf, and dried thyme.
5. Simmer until the vegetables are tender.
6. Return the cooked chicken to the pot and heat

through.

7. Season the chowder with salt and black pepper to taste.
8. Garnish with chopped fresh parsley before serving.

Recipe 2: Spinach and Potato Chowder
Ingredients:

- 2 cups of diced potatoes
- 1 onion, finely chopped
- 2 cloves of garlic, minced
- 4 cups of vegetable broth (low-sodium)
- 2 cups of fresh spinach, chopped
- 1 cup of skim milk
- 1/2 teaspoon of dried thyme
- Salt and black pepper to taste
- Chopped green onions for garnish

Instructions:

1. In a large pot, sauté the chopped onion and minced garlic until translucent.
2. Add the diced potatoes and sauté for a few minutes.
3. Pour in the vegetable broth and dried thyme.
4. Simmer until the potatoes are tender.
5. Stir in the fresh spinach and cook until wilted.
6. Add the skim milk and heat through.
7. Season the chowder with salt and black pepper to taste.
8. Garnish with chopped green onions before serving.

These lighter, broth-based chowder recipes allow you to savor the comforting flavors of chowder while embracing a healthier and more nutritious option. By incorporating fresh vegetables and making smart ingredient choices, you can enjoy a satisfying bowl of chowder without guilt.

Chapter 13: Chowder for All Seasons

In this chapter, we'll celebrate the versatility of chowder by exploring how to enjoy it in every season. You'll discover the beauty of seasonal ingredients and variations, find creative summer chowder recipes with a twist, and cozy up with winter warmers that will keep you warm and satisfied.

Seasonal Ingredients and Variations

One of the joys of chowder is its adaptability to the seasons. Here are some ideas for making the most of seasonal ingredients:

Spring: Spring chowders can feature fresh peas, asparagus, and tender young potatoes. Consider using leeks and spring onions for a mild onion flavor. A touch of fresh herbs like chives or tarragon adds vibrancy.

Summer: Summer chowders burst with the flavors of ripe tomatoes, corn, zucchini, and bell peppers. Fresh herbs like basil or cilantro can provide a burst of freshness. Don't forget to explore seafood options like crab or shrimp for a coastal twist.

Fall: As the weather cools, embrace autumn's bounty with ingredients like butternut squash, sweet potatoes, and hearty kale. Earthy herbs like rosemary and thyme complement the season's flavors.

Winter: Winter chowders are all about comfort and warmth. Consider incorporating root vegetables like carrots and parsnips, along with winter greens like Swiss chard or kale. Creamy, hearty chowders with a hint of smokiness are perfect for chilly evenings.

Summer Chowders with a Twist

Here's a recipe for a creative summer chowder with a twist:

Recipe: Spicy Mexican Street Corn Chowder
Ingredients:

- 4 cups of fresh corn kernels (about 4-5 ears of corn)
- 1 red bell pepper, diced
- 1 jalapeño pepper, minced (adjust to taste)
- 1 onion, finely chopped
- 2 cloves of garlic, minced
- 4 cups of vegetable broth (low-sodium)
- 1 cup of diced tomatoes (canned or fresh)
- 1 teaspoon of chili powder
- Juice of 1 lime
- 1/2 cup of fresh cilantro, chopped
- Salt and black pepper to taste
- Crumbled cotija cheese and lime wedges for garnish (optional)

Instructions:

1. In a large pot, sauté the chopped onion, minced garlic, and diced red bell pepper in olive oil until softened.
2. Add the fresh corn kernels and jalapeño pepper. Sauté for a few minutes until the corn begins to caramelize and develop a charred flavor.
3. Pour in the vegetable broth, diced tomatoes, and chili powder. Simmer for about 15-20 minutes.
4. Use an immersion blender to partially puree the chowder while leaving some chunks for texture.
5. Stir in the lime juice and chopped fresh cilantro.
6. Season with salt and black pepper to taste.
7. Serve garnished with crumbled cotija cheese and lime

wedges if desired.

Cozy Winter Warmers

Here's a recipe for a comforting winter chowder:

Recipe: Creamy Butternut Squash and Kale Chowder

Ingredients:

- 2 cups of diced butternut squash
- 1 onion, finely chopped
- 2 cloves of garlic, minced
- 4 cups of vegetable broth (low-sodium)
- 2 cups of chopped kale
- 1 cup of diced potatoes
- 1/2 teaspoon of dried rosemary
- 1/4 teaspoon of smoked paprika
- 1 cup of almond milk (or any plant-based milk)
- Salt and black pepper to taste
- Chopped fresh parsley for garnish

Instructions:

1. In a large pot, sauté the chopped onion and minced garlic in olive oil until translucent.
2. Add the diced butternut squash, potatoes, dried rosemary, and smoked paprika. Sauté for a few minutes.
3. Pour in the vegetable broth and simmer until the vegetables are tender.
4. Stir in the chopped kale and cook until wilted.
5. Use an immersion blender to puree the chowder until

smooth.

6. Return the chowder to the pot, add the almond milk, and heat through.
7. Season with salt and black pepper to taste.
8. Garnish with chopped fresh parsley before serving.

These seasonal chowder variations demonstrate the versatility of this beloved dish. By embracing the flavors and ingredients of each season, you can enjoy chowder year-round and savor the best that every season has to offer.

Chapter 14: Perfect Chowder Pairings: Breads and Crackers

In this chapter, we'll delve into the art of pairing chowder with the perfect breads and crackers. You'll discover classic options, explore homemade bread recipes, and learn how to pair chowder with unique and delightful bread choices that elevate your chowder experience.

Classic Bread and Cracker Options

Saltine Crackers: Saltines are a timeless and simple choice. Their crisp texture and mild saltiness complement the creamy richness of chowder.

Oyster Crackers: These small, round crackers are a classic accompaniment to chowder, and their name alone hints at their affinity for seafood chowders.

Sourdough Bread: Sourdough's tangy flavor and chewy texture make it an excellent choice. It's perfect for dipping and adds a delightful contrast to the creaminess of the chowder.

French Baguette: A crusty baguette is a versatile option. Slice it into thin rounds or tear off chunks to soak up the chowder.

Cornbread: Cornbread's sweet and savory flavors complement chowder, particularly when it includes corn kernels for added texture.

Homemade Bread Recipes

If you're feeling adventurous or want to impress your guests, consider making homemade bread to pair with your chowder. Here are two recipes:

Recipe 1: Homemade Sourdough Bread
Ingredients:

- 1 cup of sourdough starter
- 1 1/2 cups of warm water
- 4 cups of bread flour
- 1 1/2 teaspoons of salt

Instructions:

1. In a large bowl, combine the sourdough starter and warm water.
2. Add the bread flour and salt, and mix until a shaggy dough forms.
3. Cover the bowl and let it rest for about 30 minutes.
4. Perform a series of fold-and-turns every 30 minutes for 2-3 hours, allowing the dough to rise.
5. Shape the dough into a round loaf, place it on a floured surface, and let it rise for another 30-60 minutes.
6. Preheat your oven to 450°F (230°C) with a Dutch oven inside.
7. Score the top of the bread, place it in the preheated Dutch oven, and cover with the lid.
8. Bake for 30 minutes with the lid on, then remove the lid and bake for an additional 15-20 minutes or until the bread is golden brown and sounds hollow when tapped.
9. Allow the bread to cool before slicing and serving with chowder.

Recipe 2: Classic Cornbread
Ingredients:

- 1 cup of cornmeal
- 1 cup of all-purpose flour
- 1/4 cup of sugar
- 1 tablespoon of baking powder
- 1/2 teaspoon of salt
- 1 cup of milk
- 1/4 cup of melted butter
- 1 large egg

Instructions:

1. Preheat your oven to 425°F (220°C) and grease an 8-inch square baking pan.
2. In a large bowl, whisk together the cornmeal, all-purpose flour, sugar, baking powder, and salt.
3. In another bowl, mix together the milk, melted butter, and egg.
4. Pour the wet ingredients into the dry ingredients and stir until just combined.
5. Pour the batter into the prepared baking pan and smooth the top.
6. Bake for 20-25 minutes or until the cornbread is golden brown and a toothpick inserted into the center comes out clean.
7. Let it cool for a few minutes before slicing and serving with chowder.

Pairing Chowder with Unique Bread Choices

For a unique twist on chowder pairings, consider these options:

Focaccia: The herb-infused, olive oil-drenched goodness of focaccia pairs wonderfully with chowder.

Cheddar and Chive Biscuits: These savory biscuits with sharp cheddar and fresh chives add a delightful flavor contrast to creamy chowder.

Pumpernickel Bread: Its earthy, dark flavor complements seafood chowders, particularly those with smoked or briny notes.

Jalapeño Cornbread: If you like a hint of heat, jalapeño cornbread is a zesty choice that adds a spicy kick to your chowder experience.

Pairing chowder with the right bread or crackers enhances the overall dining experience, offering a satisfying interplay of textures and flavors. Whether you opt for a classic choice or experiment with homemade bread recipes, the perfect pairing can elevate your chowder to a culinary masterpiece.

Chapter 15: Chowder in the Slow Cooker

In this chapter, we'll dive into the world of slow cooker chowders, where convenience meets comfort. You'll learn how to create delicious chowders in your slow cooker with ease, discover valuable tips and tricks for slow cooking success, and explore crowd-pleasing slow cooker chowder recipes that are sure to satisfy.

Set It and Forget It: Slow Cooker Chowders

The beauty of slow cooker chowders lies in their simplicity. With minimal effort, you can enjoy a hearty bowl of chowder that's been gently simmering and developing flavors throughout the day. Here's why slow cooker chowders are worth trying:

Convenience: You can prep your ingredients in the morning, set your slow cooker, and come home to a hot and ready meal.

Flavor Development: Slow cooking allows flavors to meld together and ingredients to become tender, resulting in a richer and more flavorful chowder.

Hands-Free Cooking: Once your ingredients are in the slow cooker, there's no need for constant monitoring or stirring.

Slow Cooker Tips and Tricks

Before we dive into recipes, here are some tips and tricks for successful slow cooker chowders:

Layer Ingredients Wisely: Place denser ingredients like potatoes and root vegetables at the bottom of the slow cooker to ensure they cook evenly.

Sauté Before Slow Cooking: For added depth of flavor, consider sautéing onions, garlic, and any aromatic vegetables in a skillet before adding them to the slow cooker.

Adjust Liquid Levels: Slow cookers don't allow for much liquid evaporation, so be mindful of the liquid levels. You may need less liquid than traditional stovetop recipes.

Use Low Heat: opt for the low heat setting to avoid overcooking delicate ingredients like seafood.

Add Dairy Last: If your recipe includes dairy products like cream or milk, add them during the final hour of cooking to prevent curdling.

Crowd-Pleasing Slow Cooker Recipes

Here are two crowd-pleasing slow cooker chowder recipes to get you started:

Recipe 1: Slow Cooker Clam Chowder

Ingredients:

- 2 cups of chopped clams (canned or fresh)
- 4 cups of diced potatoes
- 1 onion, finely chopped
- 2 cloves of garlic, minced
- 4 cups of chicken or vegetable broth (low-sodium)
- 1 cup of whole milk or half-and-half
- 2 bay leaves
- Salt and black pepper to taste
- Chopped fresh parsley for garnish

Instructions:

1. In a skillet, sauté the chopped onion and minced garlic until translucent.
2. Place the sautéed onion and garlic, diced potatoes, chopped clams, broth, and bay leaves in the slow cooker.
3. Cook on low heat for 6-8 hours or until the potatoes are tender.
4. During the last hour of cooking, stir in the whole milk or half-and-half.
5. Season the chowder with salt and black pepper to taste.
6. Remove the bay leaves and discard them.
7. Garnish with chopped fresh parsley before serving.

Recipe 2: Slow Cooker Corn and Bacon Chowder

Ingredients:

- 4 cups of corn kernels (fresh or frozen)
- 1 onion, finely chopped
- 2 cloves of garlic, minced
- 8 slices of bacon, cooked and crumbled
- 4 cups of chicken or vegetable broth (low-sodium)
- 2 cups of diced potatoes
- 1 cup of heavy cream
- 1 teaspoon of dried thyme
- Salt and black pepper to taste
- Chopped chives and shredded cheddar cheese for garnish

Instructions:

1. In a skillet, sauté the chopped onion and minced garlic until translucent.
2. Place the sautéed onion and garlic, corn kernels, crumbled bacon, broth, diced potatoes, and dried thyme in the slow cooker.
3. Cook on low heat for 6-8 hours or until the potatoes are tender.
4. During the last hour of cooking, stir in the heavy cream.
5. Season the chowder with salt and black pepper to taste.
6. Serve garnished with chopped chives and shredded cheddar cheese.

Slow cooker chowders offer a hassle-free way to enjoy this comforting dish without constant supervision. With the right techniques and recipes, you can create hearty and flavorful chowders that will delight your taste buds and those of your guests.

Chapter 16: One-Pot Chowder Wonders

In this chapter, we'll explore the world of one-pot chowders, where simplicity meets deliciousness. You'll learn how to create fantastic chowder dishes with minimal cleanup, making them ideal for quick and easy weeknight meals.

Simplifying Chowder with One-Pot Recipes

One-pot chowders are all about convenience. By combining all the ingredients in a single pot, you can simplify the cooking process and reduce the number of dishes you need to clean. Here's why one-pot chowders are so appealing:

Efficiency: You'll save time on both cooking and cleanup, making one-pot chowders perfect for busy weeknights.

Flavor Infusion: Cooking all the ingredients together allows flavors to meld and develop, resulting in a rich and harmonious chowder.

Versatility: One-pot chowders are highly adaptable, allowing you to experiment with different ingredients and flavors while keeping the process streamlined.

Minimizing Cleanup

To make the most of one-pot chowders and minimize cleanup, consider these tips:

Prep Ingredients First: Before you start cooking, gather and prep all your ingredients. This includes chopping vegetables, measuring out spices, and having all the necessary components at the ready.

Use the Right Pot: Choose a pot or Dutch oven large enough to comfortably hold all your ingredients without overflowing.

Layer Ingredients Wisely: Place denser ingredients at the bottom of the pot and layer accordingly to ensure even cooking.

Stir Occasionally: While one-pot chowders require less attention than traditional stovetop cooking, it's essential to stir occasionally to prevent sticking or burning.

Quick and Easy Weeknight Meals

Here are two delicious one-pot chowder recipes that make for quick and easy weeknight meals:

Recipe 1: One-Pot Chicken and Corn Chowder

Ingredients:

- 2 boneless, skinless chicken breasts, diced
- 1 onion, finely chopped
- 2 cloves of garlic, minced
- 2 cups of diced potatoes
- 2 cups of fresh or frozen corn kernels
- 4 cups of chicken broth (low-sodium)
- 1 cup of whole milk or half-and-half
- 1 bay leaf
- 1/2 teaspoon of dried thyme
- Salt and black pepper to taste
- Chopped fresh chives for garnish

Instructions:

1. In a large pot or Dutch oven, sauté the diced chicken until cooked through. Remove it from the pot and set it aside.
2. In the same pot, sauté the chopped onion and minced garlic until translucent.
3. Add the diced potatoes, corn kernels, chicken broth, bay leaf, and dried thyme to the pot.
4. Simmer until the potatoes are tender.
5. Return the cooked chicken to the pot and heat through.
6. Stir in the whole milk or half-and-half.

7. Season the chowder with salt and black pepper to taste.
8. Remove the bay leaf and discard it.
9. Garnish with chopped fresh chives before serving.

Recipe 2: One-Pot Vegan Potato Leek Chowder
Ingredients:

- 2 leeks, white and light green parts, thinly sliced
- 3 cups of diced potatoes
- 4 cups of vegetable broth (low-sodium)
- 1 cup of almond milk (or any plant-based milk)
- 1 bay leaf
- 1/2 teaspoon of dried thyme
- Salt and black pepper to taste
- Chopped fresh dill for garnish

Instructions:

1. In a large pot or Dutch oven, sauté the sliced leeks in olive oil until softened.
2. Add the diced potatoes, vegetable broth, bay leaf, and dried thyme to the pot.
3. Simmer until the potatoes are tender.
4. Remove the bay leaf and discard it.
5. Use an immersion blender to partially puree the chowder, leaving some chunks for texture.
6. Stir in the almond milk and heat through.
7. Season the chowder with salt and black pepper to taste.
8. Garnish with chopped fresh dill before serving.

One-pot chowders are a game-changer for weeknight cooking. With minimal cleanup and maximum flavor, these recipes are perfect for those evenings when you want a hearty and satisfying meal without the fuss.

Chapter 17: Clam Chowder Around the World

In this chapter, we'll embark on a culinary journey to explore clam chowder variations from around the world. You'll discover international adaptations of this beloved dish, delve into global chowder traditions, and learn how to bring international flavors into your own kitchen.

International Variations on Chowder

Chowder isn't exclusive to New England; it has inspired diverse interpretations worldwide. Here are some international chowder variations:

Manhattan Clam Chowder (New York, USA): This tomato-based chowder is known for its vibrant red color and features a medley of clams, tomatoes, vegetables, and sometimes bacon.

Corn and Clam Chowder (Southern United States): A delightful Southern twist, this chowder combines clams with sweet corn, often incorporating ingredients like smoked sausage or andouille for added flavor.

Seafood Chowder (Maritime Canada): In the Canadian Maritimes, seafood chowder is a cherished dish. It typically features a combination of clams, lobster, scallops, and fish in a creamy base.

Bouillabaisse (Provence, France): Bouillabaisse is a flavorful Mediterranean fish stew, featuring a variety of seafood such as fish, mussels, and clams, simmered in a tomato-based broth with aromatic herbs and spices.

Caldeirada (Portugal): Caldeirada is a Portuguese fish stew, often including clams, white fish, and potatoes, flavored with herbs, paprika, and white wine.

Exploring Global Chowder Traditions

To truly understand the essence of global chowder traditions, it's essential to explore not only the ingredients but also the culinary culture and history behind each dish. Here are some key aspects to consider:

Local Ingredients: Different regions have access to distinct seafood and produce, influencing the ingredients used in their chowders.

Cooking Techniques: The methods of preparation and cooking can vary, from slow simmering to quick sautéing.

Flavor Profiles: Each chowder has its unique flavor profile, whether it's the tomato-based tang of Manhattan clam chowder or the rich creaminess of New England clam chowder.

Serving Traditions: Some chowders are enjoyed as everyday meals, while others are reserved for special occasions or festivals.

Bringing International Flavors to Your Kitchen

You can bring the flavors of global chowder traditions to your own kitchen by experimenting with various ingredients and techniques. Here are some ideas:

Try Different Seafood: Explore the seafood available in your area and incorporate it into your chowder. Experiment with combinations like shrimp, crab, or squid.

Use Local Produce: Infuse regional flavors into your chowder by incorporating locally sourced vegetables and herbs.

Experiment with Spices: Experiment with spices and seasonings commonly used in international cuisines to add depth and complexity to your chowder.

Incorporate Unique Ingredients: Consider incorporating unique ingredients like saffron, chorizo, or coconut milk for a twist on traditional chowder.

Learn Regional Techniques: Study the cooking techniques used in different chowder traditions and adapt them to your recipes.

By embracing global chowder traditions, you can expand your culinary horizons and create chowders that celebrate the diverse flavors of the world.

Chapter 18: Chowder for Entertaining: Party-Sized Portions

In this chapter, we'll explore how to make chowder fit for entertaining a crowd. You'll learn how to scale up classic recipes, discover presentation and buffet ideas, and get tips on hosting a chowder-themed party that will leave your guests impressed and satisfied.

Scaling Up Classic Recipes

When it comes to serving chowder to a larger group, it's essential to scale up your recipes effectively. Here's a basic guide to help you:

Calculate Servings: Determine how many servings you'll need based on the number of guests. Classic recipes typically serve 4-6 people, so multiply the ingredients accordingly.

Use a Large Pot: Invest in a larger pot or Dutch oven to accommodate the increased quantity of ingredients. Ensure it's large enough to stir comfortably.

Maintain Ratios: Pay attention to ingredient ratios. While you're increasing the quantity, try to maintain the same ratio of clams, vegetables, broth, and seasonings to maintain the intended flavor profile.

Taste and Adjust: As you cook, taste your chowder and adjust seasonings as needed. Larger batches may require more seasoning than small ones.

Keep It Warm: To keep your chowder warm and ready for serving, consider using a slow cooker or chafing dish, especially if you're hosting a buffet-style gathering.

Presentation and Buffet Ideas

Presentation is key when entertaining with chowder. Here are some presentation and buffet ideas:

Soup Tureens: Serve chowder in elegant soup tureens or large, decorative pots for a touch of sophistication.

Individual Cups: For a more casual gathering, provide smaller cups or bowls so guests can help themselves to individual servings.

Garnish Bar: Create a garnish station with a variety of toppings like chopped scallions, crumbled bacon, grated cheese, and oyster crackers. Allow guests to customize their chowder.

Bread Baskets: Offer a selection of bread and crackers in baskets, so guests can pair their chowder with their choice of carbs.

Chowder Shooters: For a unique presentation, serve chowder in shot glasses or small cups as appetizers or part of a tasting menu.

Hosting a Chowder-Themed Party

If you want to take your chowder entertaining to the next level, consider hosting a chowder-themed party. Here's how:

Invitations: Send out themed invitations that set the tone for the event, whether it's a beachside clam bake or an elegant chowder soiree.

Variety of Chowders: Offer a selection of chowders, including classics like New England clam chowder and Manhattan clam chowder, as well as some unique global variations.

Signature Drinks: Pair your chowders with signature cocktails, mocktails, or wine pairings that complement the flavors of the chowder.

Decor: Decorate your space to match the theme. Consider nautical decor, beach-inspired centerpieces, or rustic elements for a cozy atmosphere.

Music: Create a playlist that matches the vibe of your party, whether it's laid-back beach tunes or jazzy standards.

Games and Activities: Plan some games or activities to keep guests entertained, like a chowder-tasting competition or beach volleyball if you're hosting a beach-themed party.

Favors: Send guests home with small favors like mini jars of homemade chowder or custom-made chowder mugs.

A chowder-themed party is a fantastic way to celebrate this comforting dish and create memorable moments with your guests. Whether you're hosting an intimate gathering or a larger event, chowder has the versatility to suit any occasion.

Chapter 19: Chowder for Kids and Picky Eaters

In this chapter, we'll explore how to make chowder appealing to kids and picky eaters. You'll discover family-friendly chowder recipes, tips for encouraging kids to try new flavors, and fun chowder toppings and dippers that make mealtime enjoyable for everyone.

Family-Friendly Chowder Recipes

Creating chowder recipes that are kid-friendly and suitable for picky eaters requires a balance of familiar flavors and wholesome ingredients. Here are some family-friendly chowder ideas:

Cheesy Potato Chowder: This creamy chowder combines diced potatoes, cheddar cheese, and a touch of bacon for a flavor that kids adore.

Chicken and Corn Chowder: Incorporate diced chicken, sweet corn, and mild spices for a chowder that's both comforting and kid-approved.

Mild Vegetable Chowder: Create a veggie-packed chowder with mild vegetables like carrots, peas, and green beans in a creamy broth.

Tomato and Pasta Chowder: This variation combines the familiarity of tomato soup with pasta shapes and diced vegetables, making it a hit with kids.

Mini Meatball Chowder: Add mini meatballs to your chowder for a fun twist on a classic. Kids love the bite-sized protein-packed addition.

Encouraging Kids to Try New Flavors

Introducing new flavors to kids can be a rewarding experience. Here are some tips for encouraging them to try new chowder variations:

Get Them Involved: Invite kids to participate in the cooking process. They may be more willing to try a dish they had a hand in making.

Offer Choice: Allow kids to choose between two chowder options or toppings. This gives them a sense of control and involvement.

Start with Familiar Ingredients: Incorporate one or two familiar ingredients in a new chowder to ease the transition to different flavors.

Creative Names: Give your chowders fun and creative names. A "Superhero Veggie Chowder" may be more appealing than "Vegetable Chowder."

Pretend Play: Encourage imaginative play by creating a story or game around the chowder. For example, they could be explorers discovering treasure in a pirate's stew.

Fun Chowder Toppings and Dippers

Adding interactive elements to chowder can make it more enjoyable for kids. Consider these fun toppings and dippers:

Mini Grilled Cheese Sandwiches: Serve mini grilled cheese sandwiches on the side for dipping into tomato-based chowders.

Cheese and Bacon Crumbles: Offer a topping bar with shredded cheese and crumbled bacon for kids to sprinkle on their chowder.

Goldfish Crackers: Float colorful goldfish crackers on top of chowder for a playful touch.

Sour Cream Smileys: Use sour cream to create smiley faces on the surface of creamy chowder.

Bread Bowls: Hollow out small bread rolls to create edible bread bowls. Kids can tear off pieces of the bowl to dip into their chowder.

Chowder Shooters: Serve chowder in shot glasses or small cups as "chowder shooters" for a playful presentation.

Making chowder appealing to kids and picky eaters involves creativity and patience. By offering familiar ingredients, involving kids in the cooking process, and adding playful elements, you can make chowder a meal that the whole family can enjoy together.

Chapter 20: Desserts Inspired by Chowder: Sweet Surprises

In this chapter, we'll explore the delightful world of desserts inspired by chowder. You'll discover sweet treats with a chowder twist, creative dessert recipes using chowder ingredients, and even chowder-inspired dessert pairings that will surprise and delight your taste buds.

Sweet Treats with a Chowder Twist

Chowder ingredients can be surprisingly versatile when used in desserts. Here are some sweet treats with a chowder twist to get your creative culinary juices flowing:

Corn Pudding: A dessert version of corn chowder, corn pudding combines corn kernels, cream, sugar, and a touch of vanilla for a comforting, custardy treat.

Clam and Chocolate Truffles: These unique truffles incorporate chopped clams into a creamy chocolate ganache for a sweet and savory fusion.

Potato Doughnuts: Inspired by potato chowder, potato doughnuts are moist and tender, with a hint of potato flavor and a dusting of cinnamon sugar.

Seafood-Inspired Fruit Compote: Create a fruity dessert with a seafood twist by simmering fruits like apples and pears with clam juice, sugar, and spices for a flavorful compote.

Bread Pudding with Oyster Crackers: Replace traditional bread with oyster crackers in a bread pudding recipe. The crackers absorb the custard and add a unique texture to this dessert.

Creative Dessert Recipes Using Chowder Ingredients

Chowder ingredients can be the secret to creating unique and flavorful desserts. Here are some creative dessert recipes to try:

Corn and Clam Ice Cream: Infuse your ice cream base with pureed corn and a clam-infused cream to create a sweet and savory ice cream experience.

Bacon and Chocolate Brownies: Add finely chopped crispy bacon bits to your brownie batter for a sweet and salty chocolate treat.

Potato Candy: Use mashed potatoes as a base for a creamy potato candy filling, which is then rolled in powdered sugar and flavored with vanilla or cocoa powder.

Clamshell Cookies: Create clamshell-shaped sugar cookies filled with a sweet cream filling for a whimsical dessert inspired by clam chowder.

Chowder-Inspired Dessert Pairings

Pairing desserts with chowder can be a delightful adventure in flavor contrasts and complements. Here are some dessert and chowder pairings to consider:

Corn Pudding with Lobster Chowder: The sweetness of corn pudding pairs beautifully with the rich and savory flavors of lobster chowder.

Chocolate Mousse with Manhattan Clam Chowder: The silky and indulgent nature of chocolate mousse balances the acidity and intensity of Manhattan clam chowder.

Potato Doughnuts with New England Clam Chowder: The soft, sweet doughnuts complement the creamy and comforting qualities of New England clam chowder.

Fruit Compote with Seafood Chowder: The fruity sweetness of the compote offers a refreshing contrast to the richness of seafood chowder.

Bacon and Chocolate Brownies with Tomato Chowder: The combination of sweet and salty in the brownies pairs wonderfully with the tomato-based tang of tomato chowder.

Desserts inspired by chowder offer a unique and unexpected twist on traditional sweets. By incorporating chowder ingredients and flavors into your desserts, you can create memorable culinary experiences that surprise and delight your guests. This concludes our exploration of chowder-inspired culinary adventures. Whether you're savoring a classic New England clam chowder or indulging in a sweet corn pudding, may your chowder journey be filled with delicious discoveries.

In this cookbook, we've embarked on a flavorful journey through the world of chowder. From the classic New England clam chowder to international variations, creative adaptations, and even dessert surprises, we've explored the versatility and richness of this beloved dish.

We've delved into the heart of chowder, uncovering the secrets of sourcing and preparing fresh clams, understanding essential ingredients and equipment, and mastering the art of crafting the perfect chowder base. We've ventured into the realm of creativity, exploring creamy versus tomato-based chowders, homemade broth, and choosing between roux and cream for thickening.

Our journey has taken us to coastal towns, where we've discovered chowder specialties from iconic destinations and learned how to capture those coastal flavors in our own kitchens. We've explored seafood medley chowders, vegetarian and vegan alternatives, and lighter, healthier options to suit every palate and dietary preference.

We've celebrated chowder in all seasons, from summer twists to cozy winter warmers, and we've paired our chowders perfectly with a variety of breads and crackers. We've even ventured into the convenience of slow cookers and one-pot wonders, making chowder accessible for busy lifestyles and entertaining guests.

The chowder journey didn't stop there. We explored chowder around the world, discovering international variations and traditions that expanded our culinary horizons. We even learned how to host chowder-themed parties and make chowder appealing to kids and picky eaters.

Finally, we added a sweet surprise to our chowder adventure by exploring dessert inspirations that use chowder ingredients and creative pairings that tantalize the taste buds.

As our culinary voyage concludes, we hope you've found inspiration, knowledge, and above all, the joy of chowder in all its forms. Whether you're savoring a bowl of traditional clam chowder on a chilly evening or surprising your guests with chowder-inspired desserts, may your culinary endeavors be filled with delicious discoveries and shared moments of delight.

Bon appétit, and happy chowder-making!